Phil H. LISTEMANN

Colour artwork: Malcolm Laird

Layout & project design: Phil Listemann

Copyright © Philedition - Phil Listemann 2011
Published in France

ISBN 978-2-9532544-4-0

All rights reserved. No parts of this publication may be reproduced, stored in a retrieval system or transmitted in any form or by any means, electronic, mechanical, photocopying, recording or otherwise, without permission in writing from the Authors.

ACKNOWLEDGEMENTS

Jim Grant (Text Consultant), Steve Mackenzie, David Vincent
Aviation Heritage Museum of WA

Edited and printed by Phil H. Listemann

philedition@wanadoo.fr

GLOSSARY OF TERMS

DFC : Distinguished Flying Cross	RAF : Royal Air Force
F/L : Flight Lieutenant	RCAF : Royal Canadian Air Force
F/O : Flying Officer	RNZAF : Royal New Zealand Air Force
F/Sgt : Flight Sergeant	(NZ)/RAAF : New Zealander serving with the RAAF
NEI : Netherland East Indies	Sgt : Sergeant
NEIAF : NEI Air Force	S/L : Squadron Leader
ORB : Operational Record Book	Sqn : Squadron
P/O : Pilot Officer	W/C : Wing Commander
PoW : Prisoner of War	W/O : Warrant Officer
RAAF : Royal Australian Air Force	

An impressive shot of a B-25J-1 of the 42nd BG flying low over the water. The "Crusader" logo is clearly painted on the tail. In 1944 this group was based in the Philippines. Note the solid nose with eight 0.50 calibre machine-guns, which were largely used in the Pacific.

INTRODUCTION

The Mitchell was ordered "off the drawing board" in September 1939, being a development of North American's NA-40 conceived in 1938. There was no XB-25 and the first of 24 B-25s made its maiden flight on 19 August 1940, powered by two 1,700 hp Cyclone engines. The B-25As which followed were similar apart from some internal improvements and 40 of this version had been completed, and were in service, at the time of the attack on Pearl Harbour. Production of the 119 B-25B, with armament changes, was under way and although this version became famous for its participation in the Tokyo raid, it was was not really combat ready. This mark was soon followed by the B-25C (built at Inglewood, California) and D (built at Kansas City, Montana) which were largely similar, apart from the engines and some internal changes. Those two versions were widely used until the end of the war and eventually 1,619 B-25Cs and 2,290 B-25Ds were completed.

The B-25 Mitchell, unlike its competitor, the Martin B-26 Marauder, was widely exported and deliveries were made to the air forces of the United Kingdom, Soviet Union, the Netherlands, Brazil, Canada and Australia. The US Marine Corps introduced its own version under the denomination of PBJ and this saw action in the Pacific. These conventional bomber versions were followed by the unconventional B-25G of which 405 were produced. This mark was equipped with the famous 75 mm cannon carried in a "solid" nose. The 1,000 B-25Hs which followed were an improved version of the B-25G which utilised a lighter version 75 mm cannon, together with fourteen 0.50 machine-guns and provision for a torpedo or 3,200 lb of bombs, making this Mitchell one of the most heavily armed aircraft in the world. However the use of the 75 mm calibre cannon was gradually discontinued during the war.

In the early weeks of 1944 a new version, the B-25J, was introduced and this became the main version of the Mitchell. This was in production from late 1943 to the end of the war and a total of 4,318 had been completed. Production was stopped after VJ-Day. This model reverted to the bombing role but apart from its transparent nose, and modified armament, it was similar to the B-25H.

Some B-25Js were subsequently modified in the field to have a "solid" eight-machine-gun nose for ground attack. The B-25 was the most used allied medium bomber during WW2 and it saw action in all fronts.

During the war the Mitchell, under the denomination of AT-24, proved that it was a good aircraft for training and nearly 1,000 Mitchells were converted to trainers after the war, while others were converted to staff transports or handed over to a number of Latin American countries which used them as bombers well into the fifties.

B-25s FOR THE RAAF

The use of the B-25 by the RAAF was directly connected to the Dutch who had ordered 162 B-25 Mitchells to replace the ageing Martin 166 bombers operated by their NEIAF squadrons based in the Netherlands East Indies.

The occupation of the Dutch colonies in the Far East, by the Japanese, in 1942 prevented any deliveries being made. Although five were sent in great haste early that year they failed to reach their destination before the NEI forces capitulated in March 1942.

Meanwhile many NEIAF airmen had been evacuated to Australia and the possibility of forming RAAF squadrons manned by the Dutch airmen was discussed, and an agreement was reached whereby two squadrons would be formed, one fighter and one bomber. These units would become NEIAF units under the full control of the RAAF.

Regarding the bomber squadron it was logical to equip this unit, No.18 (NEI) Squadron, with the Mitchell as they had been paid for and the Dutch did not want them charged to their Lend-Lease account in the USA. The first Mitchells to have been taken on charge by the Dutch arrived in April 1942, on loan from USAAF. Over the following years no less than 150 B-25s were delivered and soon the number of aircraft available became too many for a single squadron to operate.

The idea of a second NEIAF bomber squadron was still-born

due to a shortage of Dutch aircrew and the NEIAF in Australia eventually transferred a number of B-25s to the RAAF, the first deliveries occurring in May 1944.

The RAAF received a mixed batch of the more recent sub-types of the B-25D and early sub-types of the J models. In all 39 NEIAF Mitchells were transferred to the RAAF to equip No.2 Squadron, the only one to operate this aircraft. All the aircraft were in good condition with low hours on their airframes, and none had seen service with No.18 (NEI) Squadron. For stores purposes the RAAF allocated the airframe number A47 to their B-25s, this prefix forming part of their serial number, and all were modified to RAAF standard.

On 23 January 1945 the Australians reached an agreement, Requisition No.43336, for a batch of brand new B-25Js to be delivered from the United States but these deliveries were terminated after the receipt of the 11th aircraft. The exact number of Lend-Leased B-25s scheduled to be supplied by the Americans is not known, but it is possible that the request was made to replace the whole fleet, which was ageing and suffered a high attrition rate, with new aircraft. In all 50 B-25s went onto the RAAF's inventory, 39 of them were taken on charge by No.2 Squadron, RAAF or used for training purposes.

THE B-25 OF THE RAAF

Serial	NEIAF	US serial	Type	TOC
A47-1	N5-183	42-87607	D-30-NC	22.04.44
A47-2	N5-187	43-3422	D-30-NC	22.04.44
A47-3	N5-181	43-3423	D-30-NC	22.04.44
A47-4	N5-189	43-3424	D-30-NC	22.04.44
A47-5	N5-192	43-3426	D-30-NC	22.04.44
A47-6	N5-193	43-3427	D-30-NC	22.04.44
A47-7	N5-194	43-3607	D-30-NC	22.04.44
A47-8	N5-195	43-3613	D-30-NC	22.04.44
A47-9	N5-196	43-3621	D-35-NC	22.04.44
A47-10	N5-197	43-3623	D-35-NC	22.04.44
A47-11	N5-198	43-3624	D-35-NC	22.04.44
A47-12	N5-199	43-3625	D-35-NC	22.04.44
A47-13	N5-200	43-3626	D-35-NC	22.04.44
A47-14	N5-201	43-3766	D-35-NC	22.04.44
A47-15	N5-202	43-3767	D-35-NC	22.04.44
A47-16	N5-203	43-3768	D-35-NC	21.04.44
A47-17	N5-204	43-3769	D-35-NC	21.04.44
A47-18	N5-205	43-3770	D-35-NC	22.04.44
A47-19	N5-206	43-3790	D-35-NC	21.04.44
A47-20	N5-207	43-3791	D-35-NC	21.04.44
A47-21	N5-213	43-3789	D-35-NC	09.06.44
A47-22	N5-190	43-3830	D-35-NC	13.06.44
A47-23	N5-212	43-3832	D-35-NC	09.06.44
A47-24	N5-216	43-3867	D-35-NC	10.06.44
A47-25	N5-215	43-3869	D-35-NC	09.06.44
A47-26	N5-220	43-27689	J-1-NC	09.06.44
A47-27	N5-219	43-27691	J-1-NC	09.06.44
A47-28	N5-224	43-27927	J-5-NC	11.07.44
A47-29	N5-225	43-27928	J-5-NC	12.07.44
A47-30	N5-229	43-28185	J-10-NC	27.07.44
A47-31	N5-231	43-28183	J-10-NC	27.07.44
A47-32	N5-227	43-28181	J-10-NC	31.07.44
A47-33	N5-175	42-87259	D-25-NC	09.08.44
A47-34	N5-186	42-87608	D-30-NC	09.08.44
A47-35	N5-168	42-87416	D-25-NC	28.08.44
A47-36	N5-171	42-87255	D-25-NC	28.08.44
A47-37	N5-174	42-87258	D-25-NC	28.08.44
A47-38	N5-232	44-29021	J-15-NC	13.07.44
A47-39	N5-235	44-29024	J-15-NC	19.09.44
A47-40	-	44-30888	J-25-NC	12.04.45
A47-41	-	44-30889	J-25-NC	13.04.45
A47-42	-	44-30890	J-25-NC	13.04.45
A47-43	-	44-30895	J-25-NC	24.04.45
A47-44	-	44-30896	J-25-NC	28.04.45
A47-45	-	44-30897	J-25-NC	01.05.45
A47-46	-	44-31255	J-30-NC	26.05.45
A47-47	-	44-31254	J-30-NC	28.05.45
A47-48	-	44-31253	J-30-NC	03.06.45
A47-49	-	44-86859	J-30-NC	19.08.45
A47-50	-	44-86855	J-30-NC	27.08.45

A formation of four Mitchells of No.18 (NEI) Squadron heading to their target. B-25D N5-188 is leading B-25Js, N5-218, N5-230 and N5-226. Although the Mitchells were purchased, and paid for, to replace the ageing Martin 139 and 166s the Dutch were never able to train enough crews for so many aircraft, which allowed them to transfer a number of surplus B-25s to the RAAF. Prior to this the RAAF had not considered the type for service. (*Jim Grant*)

B-25J A47-30, a former Dutch aircraft. Like all ex-Dutch aircraft it was painted in Olive Drab and Light Grey paint. This B-25J was never issued to No.2 Squadron, however the forward fuselage blister gun has been fired as can be testified by the stain left by the powder.
(*Aviation Heritage Museum of WA*)

Technical Data
B-25J (NA-108)

Manufacturer and production:
4,318 by North American (Kansas City, KS)

Type:
land-based medium bomber.

Accomodation:
Five : Pilot, Second Pilot, Bombardier/nose gunner, Navigator/radio operator, Gunner (turret).

Power plants:
Two Wright R-2600-29 fourteen-cylinder radial air-cooled (2 rows) rated 1,700 hp

Fuel & Oil
Fuel (US Gal):
Main tanks : 670 [2 535 l]
Auxiliary tanks : 304 [1 150 l]
Bomb bay droppable tank : 585 [2 215 l]

Oil (US Gal):
Standard per engine : 37.5 [142 l]

Dimensions:
Span : 67 ft 7-in [20,60 m]
Length : 53 ft 5-in [16,28 m]
Height : 16 ft 4-in [4,98 m]
Wing area : 609.7 Sq ft [56,7 m²]

Weights:
Empty : 19,500 lb [8 845 kg]
Gross : 35,000 lb [15 875 kg]

Performance:
Max speed :
272 mph at 13,000 ft
[438 km/h à 2 300 m]

Cruising speed : 230 mph [370 km/h]

Service ceiling : 29,000 ft [8 850 m]

Normal range : 1,500 miles [2 400 km]

Armament:
2 x 0.50-in [12.7 mm] in the nose with 300 rounds (one fixed, one flexible).
2 x 0.50-in [12.7mm] in blister packs on each side with 400 rpg.
2 x 0.50-in [12.7mm] in dorsal turret with 400 rpg.
1 x 0.50-in [12.7mm] each in waist position with 200 rpg.
2 x 0.50-in [12.7mm] in tail turret with 300 rpg.

provision for :
3,000 lb [2 176 kg] of bombs in the bomb bay

Deliveries and Strenght

Month (at last day)	Transferred	Total transferred	Op. Losses	Accident	SOC	**On Hand**
April 44	20	20	-	-	-	**20**
May 44	7	27	-	-	-	**27**
June 44	6	33	-	1	-	**32**
July 44	5	38	-	-	-	**37**
August 44	1	39	-	1	-	**37**
September 44	-	39	3	-	-	**34**
October 44	-	39	-	-	-	**34**
November 44	-	39	1	-	-	**33**
December 44	-	39	3	2	-	**28**
January 45	-	39	-	-	-	**28**
February 45	-	39	-	-	-	**28**
March 45	-	39	-	-	-	**28**
April 45	5	44	-	-	-	**33**
May 45	3	47	-	-	-	**36**
June 45	1	48	-	-	-	**37**
July 45	-	48	-	-	-	**37**
August 45	2	50	-	1	1	**37**
September 45	-	50	-	1	-	**36**
October 45	-	50	-	2	-	**34**
.../...						
December 46	-	50	-	-	1	**33**
.../...						
March 50	-	50	-	-	33	-

Another B-25J which was never issued, A47-44 is seen here while banking to the left during a test flight. This aircraft, left in natural metal, belongs to the batch received directly from the Americans under the Lend-Lease agreement. *(Aviation Heritage Museum of WA)*

A No.2 Squadron Mitchell, coded KO-G, in the early stages of the Australian use of the type. Note that all B-25D models had a modified tail turret.
(Nelson Hill via D. Vincent)

THE UNITS

No.2 Squadron
code : KO
April 1944 - January 1946

The RAAF unit, and eventually the only RAAF one, to operate the B-25 was No.2 Squadron. This unit, which had existed during WW1, was reformed in 1937.

Since the beginning of the Second World War the squadron had been very active in the front line having flown Ansons, Hudsons and Beauforts before converting to Mitchells, which it operated until the war's end.

On 22 May 1944 No.2 Squadron flew its last Beaufort sortie and was withdrawn from operations to convert to its new aircraft, however it remained at Hughes, the base from which the squadron had been operating since April 1943. The squadron was under the command of Wing Commander Les A. Ingram, a regular Air Force officer, who had previously served with Nos.14, 13 and 100 Squadrons RAAF. Mitchells brought about many changes in flying and operational procedures and the crews had to learn to work with a six man crew instead of four, which was the the usual number for a Beaufort crew. The newcomers were a second pilot and a tail gunner.

A first batch of 20 B-25Ds was collected from the Dutch on 21 and 22 April 1944 and with them came three Dutch pilots from No.18 (NEI) Squadron to help No.2 Squadron's pilots through the conversion. However the Australians had considerable experience on twin-engined aircraft and, as the Mitchell was easy to fly, the conversion was completed without any major incident and the squadron became operational in less than three weeks. However Mitchell A47-20 was damaged in an accident on 17 May 1944. When the pilot, Flight Lieutenant Nelson Hill, was preparing to land it was discovered that the undercarriage would not go down due to the complete failure of the hydraulic system and there was no alternative but to belly land the aircraft. While this was successful the Mitchell had to be sent back for repair and was the victim of a ground accident on 1 June which resulted in it being converted to components.

MITCHELL'S DEBUT

The RAAF now having two B-25 units under its command, operated both of them under the authority of No.79 Wing, but for a time the Dutch squadron was based at Truscott. The first operational sortie was a search mission on which two Mitchells were dispatched on 11 June 1944. The first to take off was Wing Commander Ingram and his crew flying A47-13 while the other B-25, A47-7, captained by Squadron Leader Alan Hayes took off five minutes later. Both aircraft returned to base after more than 5 hours in the air. On 23 June Squadron Leader Loneragan arrived to replace Squadron Leader Hayes who was then posted south on completion of his tour. Squadron Leader Loneragan arrived in time for the B-25's first offensive mission on 27 June 1944. The target was the landing strip of Lautem West (Timor), and nine Mitchells led by Flight Lieutenant Nelson Hill were involved in this action. Each aircraft dropped seven 500 lb bombs from 10,000 feet and despite moderate to heavy ack-ack encountered over the target all aircraft returned to base safely. The following day a bombing and strafing mission was carried out on Doka-Barat airstrip with the formation being led by Flying Officer Joe Simpson in A47-16. On the last day of June a shipping sweep was carried out by three Mitchells led by Squadron Leader Joe Lee (A47-3) after a fourth aircraft A47-7, to have been flown by Flying Officer Fileman, had to be withdrawn from the mission at the last minute. One auxiliary sloop was strafed and left sinking and this was the first success to be recorded by an Australian Mitchell.

In July, anti-shipping sweeps continued to be carried out. On the 4th, three Mitchells led by Flight Lieutenant John Ditchburn and crew (A47-13) attacked a 600 tons vessel not far from Kai Islands. Bombs were dropped without any results and the 5,500 rounds of ammunition fired at it did not achieve any better result. The vessel continued its way even though smoke was seen rising from its superstructure. The vessel was able to escape a second attack due to the onset of darkness. The same day Squadron Leader Loneragan left the squadron, on posting to No.1 Squadron, while Squadron Leader Lee was appointed in temporary command of the squadron when Wing Commander Ingram left the squadron a few days later on completion of his tour. The new CO, Wing Commander D.W.I. Campbell, who was one of the first RAAF pilots to win a DFC in the war against Japanarrived on the 11th and officially took command of the squadron on the 20th. Meanwhile the squadron was able to record another success on the 15th when a motorised barge was sunk. On 19 July, during another shipping sweep, A47-15 (Pilot Officer Arthur Pierce) was damaged by flak and the navigator, Warrant Officer 'Paddy' Ryan and the side gunner, Warrant Officer Vic Muir were wounded, but sadly the squadron had to record its first loss when Warrant Officer Ian McCallum the turret gunner was killed. Later that day another raid was conducted north of Dili and yet another Mitchell A47-15 (Flight Sergeant Peter Hocking), was hit, and Flight Sergeant Jack Purcell, one of the gunners, was injured. However the attack against the ships was not in vain as one was sunk by Sergeant Hocking who was awarded a DFM for this action. From that time onwards No.2 Squadron regularly flew in joint operations with the Dutch Mitchells of No.18 (NEI) Squadron. At the end of the month the situation of the unit was not the best as it had only 17 Mitchells on strength, out of an establishment of 20 aircraft, of which only twelve were serviceable.

First Losses

In August more combined operations were conducted in conjunction with the Dutch. On 2 August an operation against Timor met with success. This raid was carried out by 27 Mitchells, including 12 aircraft flown by the Australian squadron. When not on operations the Australians continued training and, during one such flight, on 6 August A47-13 flown by Flying Officer Stan Davies experienced difficulty in releasing its bombs while carrying out medium level formation bombing practice on a range. It appears that after the bombs had been released one exploded beneath the aircraft setting it on fire. The B-25 crash landed in a wooded area 10 miles east of Adelaide River and was completely destroyed. Four men, including Flying Officer K.J. Hadley, one of No.549 Squadron's officers who had been flying as an observer, were killed outright. The other crew members, including the captain, were admitted to hospital badly burned and in a state of shock. The navigator, Pilot Officer David Lane, died four days later from his injuries and the second pilot, Pilot Officer Arthur Buckland, passed away on 19 August. This was the first Mitchell loss sustained by the RAAF. The squadron carried out about 120 sorties during the month which were mainly shipping sweeps. However some conventional attacks were organised including one on Langgoer airfield by 11 Mitchells on 26 August, which was led by Flight Lieutenant Philip Squires. This mission called for a maximum effort from No.2 Squadron and although two Mitchells were hit by anti aircraft fire all the aircraft made it back, and no member of the crews was injured.

September began with a raid carried out in the early hours of the 1st by eight Mitchells led by the CO, Wing Commander Campbell, in co-ordination with the Dutch squadron. The raid soon proved to be a dramatic one for the squadron when A47-12, flown by Flight Lieutenant W.A. 'Tige' Carter, was posted missing. The aircraft had been damaged by flak and developed a fuel leak. When his flight instruments also failed Carter realised that he would not be able to return to base so he ditched the aircraft near a beach on Peron Islands, which resulted in the tail gunner being injured but the rest of the crew was safe and all returned later to the squadron. In addition No.18 (NEI) Squadron lost N5-214 flown by Lieutenant Drecher. The following day a rescue mission was launched to find A47-12 and one of the aircraft, A47-6, was forced to ditch near Peron Islands. Flight Lieutenant Easton, a Chaplain who was on

Three B-25s flying in formation in the early stages of its operational service in No.2 Squadron. Here A47-14/KO-F is shown in the standard camouflage inherited from the Dutch with markings painted on RAAF Mitchells at the beginning of their operational service. *(Harry Rosenhain via D. Vincent)*

board as a passenger, was killed while Warrant Officer King, a ground crewman who volunteered to participate in the search, was posted missing. The rest of the crew of A47-6 were rescued by boat.

Despite these losses the war continued and on 5 September a joint operation was carried out in conjunction with Spitfire VIIIs from No.1 Fighter Wing of the RAAF. The operation called for a single Mitchell, in this case A47-21 flown by Flying Officer Les Ekert and his crew, was to escort, and give navigational aid to, four Spitfires from each squadron (Nos. 54, 548 & 549), with two Spitfires from No.1 Fighter Wing, to strike an enemy camp close to Lingat village on Selaroe Island located south of Saumlaki. After the Spitfires had strafed the enemy camp the Mitchell dropped its four 500-lb incendiary bombs despite the heavy anti-aircraft fire which directed at the it.

Shipping patrols and sweeps remained the main task during September, occasionally alternating with armed reconnaissance sorties or strikes on land targets.

However it was during a shipping sweep on 22 September that No.2 Squadron lost its third Mitchell of the month. That day, during a shipping sweep along the north coast of Timor, A47-3 flown by Flying Officer Alan. Slater was believed to have been hit by ground fire and crashed into the sea while attacking a barge. The six men on board were killed instantly.

The rest of the month was busy with nearly 40 sorties being carried out and for the first time since June the Australians carried out more sorties than the Dutch squadron.

Bad Servicibility

October was a very busy month, not because of the level of sorties but because of an intensive training programme. New aircrew, who had just arrived to replace the tour-expired crews, had to be trained by No.2 Squadron as there was no RAAF B-25 training unit, fortunately all the new airmen had accumulated some time on Hudsons. As the Dutch and Australian squadrons of No.79 Wing had to convert all of their crews to Mitchells 'in house' this directly affected the number of combat operations which could be flown. Furthermore it shortened the time between airframe and engine overhauls and wore out the aircraft more quickly than normal. By the end of the month the number of serviceable aircraft had dropped to 8 out of an establishment of 20 and the number of sorties had been cut to one third! This low number of serviceable aircraft was also partially due to operational activity as some aircraft were being damaged on operations. For example on the 10th A47-22 (Flying Officer Robert M. Ingram) was able to return safely to the base but the aircraft was unserviceable for the next six weeks. October was generally uneventful due to a lack of enemy targets to attack.

Now that new crews had become operational the number of sorties increased, in November, to the normal level and about 100 sorties were carried out that month. After weeks of anti-shipping missions the Japanese were suffering heavily from attacks by the Dutch and Australian B-25s and only small craft were now being regularly encountered. Despite this, danger was still present on every mission and A47-8 was shot down by ground fire on the 4th. The Mitchell, flown by Flight

Masthead attack training for KO-E in August 1944. The vessel serving as the "target" is a Fairmile Type B ML807.
(P.T. Sanders via D. Vincent)

Lieutenant Jack H. Selway, was hit in the starboard engine while strafing some barges. The pilot tried to pull up but it was too late, the aircraft rolled and dived into the sea in flames giving the crew no chance of survival. Two days later the Australians, during a co-ordinated attack involving four No.2 Squadron Mitchells and twelve more from No.18 (NEI) Squadron, had their revenge when they badly damaged a 300 ton ship. During the month the Mitchells concentrated their anti-shipping activities in the Flores-Timor area with excellent results and no less than 32 vessels, including four freighters, were reported damaged or sunk and additionally, on 28 November, they sank an 80 ton vessel. A change of command the same day occurred when Wing Commander D.W.I. Campbell was replaced by Wing Commander T.S. Inglesew, a permanent air force officer. However aircraft and spare parts were in short supply and almost half of the aircraft were unserviceable.

A B-25D, coded KO-U, flying to its target in 1944. The serial cannot be read in full, the last digit being hidden, but this Mitchell could be either A47-22 or A47-23. (*Bob Horne via D. Vincent*)

On 5 December three Mitchells took off for a shipping sweep not far from the north coast of Timor. While over Laga on the north coast of the island A47-11 (Flight Lieutenant Norriss and crew) was holed by heavy machine gun or 20 mm cannon fire causing damage. Fuel was seen pouring from the trailing edge of the starboard wing and the pilot immediately feathered the propeller and stopped the starboard engine to prevent this catching fire. However A47-11's problems continued when the generator on the port engine failed making it impossible to transfer fuel from the starboard fuel tanks to the port wing tanks. It was then obvious that the aircraft would not be able to return to its base but it got as far as Bathurst Island before the fuel ran out and the port engine stopped. Flight Lieutenant Norriss made a successful crash landing despite being unable to use the flaps as the hydraulic system had also failed. Fortunately none of the crew were injured.

On 20 December A47-33 (Flight Lieutenant W.F.E. Thompson and crew) was detailed to carry out a shipping reconnaissance but they failed to return from this sortie. Post-war it was established that the Mitchell had been shot down by anti-aircraft gunfire at Saumlaki. There were no survivors and among the missing aircrew was Warrant Officer J.E.S. Thompson a New Zealander serving with the RAAF. Six days later two other Mitchells were lost. A47-9, being flown by Flying Officer Bob Avery, was one of a formation of four aircraft ordered to take part in a strike against enemy shipping near the Lucipara Islands. This aircraft was number 3 to take off and the two previous aircraft took abnormally long runs before becoming airborne, having had to use extra boost in doing so. Flying Officer Avery was less fortunate and crashed just past the end of the runway, but the crew escaped unhurt. The aircraft was burnt out and the bombs exploded throwing pieces of metal 400 metres in all directions. This however was not the end of the Australians' problems for the day as the rest of the formation led by Flight Lieutenant Ekert in A47-2 had continued the mission and attacked a 300 ton vessel near the Lucipara Islands and left it severely damaged. On the way back A47-2 was caught by a storm. Flight Lieutenant Ekert commenced his landing circuit but as he came down to 50 feet the visibility dramatically deteriorated. Ekert had no option but to continue his landing and the aircraft overshot the runway and crashed. With two Mitchells lost that day the Australians had suffered a 50% loss rate without any direct enemy action. A47-9 and A47-2 were the last two Mitchells lost during an operational flight this month and in all no less than four No.2 Squadron Mitchells were lost in December for 108 sorties. These losses could be considered high if compared with the results, four freighters and 25 smaller vessels claimed as destroyed by No.79 Wing while, in the same time, the Dutch lost one Mitchell only, N5-167, in 82 sorties.

Out of the Game

In January 1945 the squadron began preparing to move with the rest of the Wing to Jacquinot Bay in eastern New Britain to provide air support for the ongoing army operations in that sector. This move had became necessary because the success of the operations carried out during the previous months by the two Mitchell squadrons had forced the Japanese to cease all shipping activities in the area of No.79 Wing's operations. The proposed move had an affect on the squadron's operations and only 100 sorties were recorded during the first two months of 1945. Meanwhile the move to New Britain was proving chaotic as the result of a lack of shipping to transport No.79 Wing to its new base at Jacquinot Bay. In addition the facilities had not yet been modified to accommodate the Mitchells. An advanced party arrived at Jacquinot Bay at the end of February and by late March nearly half of the ground staff and most of the squadron's ground equipment had left Hughes, however at that time the advance of the American forces in the area obliged the Dutch authorities to request No.79 Wing be used on Dutch territory. Indeed it was politically important for the Dutch to have their two units, No.18 (NEI) Squadron, and No.120 (NEI) Squadron, with its P-40s, which had recently arrived to join the Wing, operate from NEI territory. In consequence, on 14 May the move to

SUGAR DIVISION (Stack Aft) 4 STACK AFT

SUGAR ABLE

Catwalks and No Hatches 7000/10500 G.T.
Foremast Centered in Forward Well 12K 19K

SUGAR BAKER

Hatches and No Catwalk 1500/2500 G.T.
Foremast usually on Forecastle 10K 13K

SUGAR CHARLIE

No Bridge Amidships 300/700 G.T.
2 Hatches, usually 2 Masts

SUGAR DOG

No Bridge Amidships 70/150 G.T.
1 Hatch, 1 Mast

SUGAR 2 STACKS

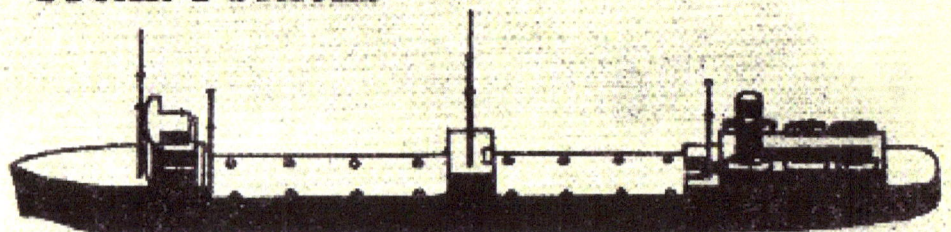

Stacks Abreast 17000/19000 G.T.
Slipway in Stern 13K 15K

Details from JAN#3 shipping recognition card dated June 1944 (perhaps to get rid of the rusty staple marks) detailing the 'Sugar' Division of Japanese shipping. "Sugar" is simply a phonetic representation of letter 'S' which in turn was meant to signify 'stacks aft', that is smokestacks aft, whilst 'Able', 'Baker', 'Charlie', 'Dog' were size indicators as shown. (D. Vincent collection).

This is the kind of craft which were regular targets for the Mitchells. They received the code name of 'Suger Charlie'. This one was attacked on 21 August by three Mitchells and was left burning as can be verified from the photograph.
(RAAF Official via David Vincent)

Jacquinot Bay was cancelled and the Wing received new orders to move to Morotai, and was assigned to the First Tactical Air Force in Borneo. Meanwhile, and before the move took place, operations continued to decrease and no operational flights were recorded in May. With a lack of targets the Mitchell crews were rarely required for operations. They were occasionally called to provide air cover for ASR searches, a mission which could be dangerous. On one such sortie, on 28 April, involving Mitchell A47-39, flown by Flight Lieutenant James Legge the aircraft was hit by ground fire while providing cover for an ASR Catalina attempting to locate the crew of a ditched Liberator.

The Japanese fire was accurate and hit the port engine which had to be shut down. Nevertheless, Legge was able to make it back to base. On 31 May the Commanding Officer, Wing Commander T.S. Ingledew, was posted south on completion of his tropical tour and was replaced by Wing Commander L.A. 'Smoky' Douglas from No.79 Wing HQ who arrived that same day.

Once again the move, this time to Borneo, was protracted. The first transfer of aircraft took place on 14 August with only six Mitchells making the trip. Regrettably one of the Mitchells was lost during this flight when they encountering heavy clouds. The formation led by Flight Lieutenant Neil Sharpe had to descend below 3,000 feet and A47-37, flown by Flight Lieutenant Edward White, was last seen disappearing behind a cloud. Meanwhile the formation had to descend to 1,000 feet and because of the clouds the formation had to split up. What happened to A47-37 is not known but the wreckage of the aircraft was found years later and it was suspected the Mitchell probably hit the hill while flying into clouds. None of the eight men on board survived. This loss, the day before the Japanese surrendered, was a bitter one for the squadron.

The squadron was reunited by end of August and, although all offensive flights had been discontinued, there was still a lot of flying to be done. Watching for Japanese activity was of great importance as no one could be sure that all the Japanese units would surrender, and some Japanese troops could well continue hostilities even after the official surrender. Reconnaissance sorties continued to be carried out with the first taking place on 19 August. This flight was made by the new CO Wing Commander L.A. Douglas and what many feared would happen occurred when his aircraft, A47-35, was hit by ground fire.

TRANSPORT AIRCRAFT

One of the Mitchells new tasks was to locate the many POW camps in the region and to drop food to them. On 15 September No.2 Squadron lost another Mitchell when A47-19, flown by Flight Lieutenant Lawrence Kirk, was detailed to escort a Catalina to Banjarmasin and drop leaflets on native villages on route. After the Catalina landed the pilot of the Mitchell flew low en the vicinity of the township apparently with the idea of impressing the natives, or the Japanese, as the attitude of both was doubtful at the time. Kirk misjudged his height and the Mitchell struck a coconut tree, crashed and burst into flames killing five of those on board on impact. Two airmen survived the crash but sadly Sergeant Fred Stolweather died a few hours later and only the tail gunner, Flight Sergeant E.A.R Booth, survived. The last operational flight was carried out on 25 September by A47-31 piloted by Flight Lieutenant George Inglis, a supply mission to Makassar. Soon after, when it became clear that the Japanese were surrendering as ordered, the ground crew removed all weapons from the Mitchells and converted them into transport aircraft. They were mainly used as a fast means of transporting Australian PoWs. On 8 October the last accident occurred when Squadron Leader D.H. Hannah fouled wing racks on edge of flare path. The aircraft, A47-23, was never repaired as the authorisation to do so was not granted due to the end of the war as the Lend-Lease Agreement obliged the Australians to pay all costs from that date.

Once this task was completed the squadron switched to

escorting the many RAAF aircraft being returned their new base, or even direct to the Air Depots, in Australia. This chapter of the squadron's activities, and the Mitchell, ended on 14 November when flying activities ceased. The squadron then began its own preparations to move back to Australia with the first airlift taking place on the 23rd. All In all No.2 Squadron, and its Mitchells, had carried out close to 1,000 sorties, 90%, of which were completed before the Japanese surrender. The cost had been high with seven B-25s lost in operations, and five others in accidents, killing a total of 44 crewmen. Compared with No.18 (NEI) Squadron for the same period, the losses sustained by No.2 Squadron were similar.

The end of the Mitchell's service was approaching and by the end of the year No.2 Squadron had been reduced to a cadre of five personnel, then the squadron was disbanded on 15 May 1946. By then the Mitchells had long gone to the storage depots as it had been not chosen to fly with the post-war RAAF, as it was a medium bomber, and the Avro Lincoln heavy bomber, which was being built in Australia, was chosen for post war service.

Second line units

Although No.2 Squadron was the only front line unit to have operated the Mitchell, some of these aircraft were also flown by second line units. The main one was the Central Flying School (CFS) based at Point Cook which was in charge of training RAAF instructors and setting standards for RAAF pilots. For this purpose four Mitchells were issued to the CFS at various times. The first two, A47-38 and 39, were delivered in October 1944, however A47-39 remained for only a month before it was issued to No.2 Squadron. A47-38, which remained until April 1946, was joined by A47-30 on 7 October 1945 and by A47-50 in January 1946. The latter remained with the CFS until May 1946 and was the last Mitchell still flying with a RAAF unit.

Prior to arriving at the CFS A47-30 had been serving with No.1 Aircraft Performance Unit (No.1 APU) since March 1945. An example of each type in service, or considered for the service, in the RAAF had to be assessed by this unit which included amongst its tasks defining the flying characteristics of each type, and production of a flight manual for use by RAAF personnel. In addition it conducted tests on modified aircraft and individual pieces of equipment. A47-30 trialled new bombsights and was used to conduct armament trials on B-25Js. A47-40, in which SCR 729 equipment had been installed, was the second aircraft to be issued to No.1 APU, but its service with this unit was short as five days later the aircraft crash-landed, just outside the airfield boundary immediately after take off, wrecking the aircraft without causing serious injuries to the crew. The pilot, Flight Lieutenant J.A.B. Boyd, had only 2.5 hours on Mitchells and his lack of experience on the type might well have been part of, if not the main cause of the accident. Otherwise all Mitchells which were not immediately issued to squadrons were held at the Air Depots, usually Nos.1 or 3 AD, where flight tests were occasionally flown to check their airworthiness. On 11 December 1944 Flight Lieutenant Robert Wines was carrying out an armament test flight in A47-24 when it caught fire and crashed into the sea off Torquay firing range. Three crew members were killed including Wines, an experienced pilot who had been awarded the DFC in 1943 while serving on Bostons with No.22 Squadron.

As the Mitchell was not selected to remain in the RAAF's post war inventory they were rapidly withdrawn from service and put into storage awaiting disposal and all surviving airframes were officially struck off charge on 1 October 1946. However they remained in storage until March 1950 when they were sold for scrap.

The Mitchell did not play a major role in the RAAF's war against Japan and having had a strong connection with the Dutch this overshadowed the Australian use of the Mitchell. Thus its impact on the RAAF's history was not significant. Nevertheless the aircraft and its crews carried out a successful war against the Japanese, as described in the first chapter, and could have accomplished much more in 1945 if things had gone differently.

Intense activity on Hughes Field in the second half of 1944. Mitchells taxiing out for the Langgoer raid on 13 August 1944.
(*Steve Mackenzie*)

THE OPERATIONAL RECORD

A47-5 was one of the first Mitchells taken on charge by No.2 Squadron and remained in service until the unit was disbanded.
(RAAF official via D. Vincent)

OPERATIONAL DIARY - NUMBER OF SORTIES

Month	Nb Sorties	Op. Hours flown
June 44	57	335.1
July 44	116	739.0
August 44	118	744.8
September 44	125	786.3
October 44	86	558.3
November 44	99	572.2
December 44	95	569.3
January 45	57	333.9
February 45	44	289.5
March 45	36	220.0
April 45	34	186.4
May 45	-	-
June 45	5	26.1
July 45	-	-
August 45	21	131.4
September 45	83	455.9
Total	**976**	**5,948.2**

Extracted from No.2 Squadron ORB

FIRST SORTIES PERFORMED

date	Mission	Serial	Time in/out
11.06.44	Search "Heron"	A47-13	0107-0614z

Crew : W/C Ingram, F/O Ekert, P/O Kaiser, W/O Bamber, F/S Robinson, F/O Knowles.

| | Search "Jackass" | A47-7/S | 0112-0658z |

Crew : S/L Hayes, F/L Cherry, F/L Brown, P/O Fletcher, P/O Hicks, Sgt Gee.

A47-7/KO-S was one of the two Mitchells which performed the first operational sorties. Below the nose art pained on A47-7 with already 22 sorties. This photo suggests that it was taken in September or October 1944.
(Steve Mackenzie)

Aircraft Lost on Operations
No.2 Squadron, RAAF

Date	Crew	Service Number	Origin	Serial/Code	Fate
01.09.44	F/L Walter A. Carter	Aus.415098	RAAF	A47-12	-
	W/O Reginald J. Pass	Aus.16940	RAAF		-
	Sgt Neville R. Elgar	Aus.409099	RAAF		-
	F/Sgt Samuel G. Moore	Aus.428049	RAAF		-
	W/O Raymond Rogers	Aus.416790	RAAF		-
	Sgt Alfred R. Batten	Aus.438308	RAAF		-
02.09.44	F/L John C. Simpson	Aus.400558	RAAF	A47-6	-
	W/O Keith R. Milligan	Aus.406945	RAAF		-
	F/O Vincent Peters	Aus.401016	RAAF		-
	F/L Alfred J. Higgins	Aus.416335	RAAF		-
	F/O Robert L. Park	Aus.418871	RAAF		-
	W/O Gordon S. King (1)	Aus.4795	RAAF		†
	F/L Hilford C. Easton (2)	Aus.423197	RAAF		†
22.09.44	F/O Allen W. Slater	Aus.414849	RAAF	A47-3	†
	F/O Murray S. Millett	Aus.426641	RAAF		†
	F/O John F. Daggett	Aus.434341	RAAF		†
	F/O Bernard A. Wisniewski	Aus.423966	RAAF		†
	F/Sgt Keith R. Philipson	Aus.429669	RAAF		†
	Sgt Desmond F. Harberger	Aus.435448	RAAF		†
04.11.44	F/O Jack H. Selway	Aus.403381	RAAF	A47-8	†
	F/O Arthur E. Pott	Aus.405932	RAAF		†
	P/O Harry B. Worman	Aus.417438	RAAF		†
	W/O John F. Stormon	Aus.415057	RAAF		†
	F/Sgt Albert E. Hawkins	Aus.418837	RAAF		†
	Sgt Richard C. Palfreyman	Aus.436941	RAAF		†
05.12.44	F/L Patrick J. Norriss	Aus.406551	RAAF	A47-11/C	-
	P/O Sydney R. Leggo	Aus.435292	RAAF		-
	F/L Philip H. Utting	Aus.415287	RAAF		-
	F/L Kenneth H. Jamieson	Aus.410160	RAAF		-
	P/O Cecil F. Lyons	Aus.405863	RAAF		-
	F/O William J. Steele (3)	Aus.412074	RAAF		-
	F/Sgt William J.E. McGee	Aus.439778	RAAF		-
20.12.44	F/O William F.E. Thompson	Aus.406741	RAAF	A47-33	†
	F/O Leslie T. Forsyth	Aus.418377	RAAF		†
	W/O John E.S. Thompson	Aus.415921	(NZ)/RAAF		†
	W/O Francis H. Mathews	Aus.418970	RAAF		†
	F/Sgt John A. Rolfe	Aus.432434	RAAF		†
	F/Sgt Thomas H. Rowlands	Aus.419918	RAAF		†
26.12.44	F/O Robert L. Avery	Aus.408360	RAAF	A47-9	-
	F/Sgt Thomas P. Lee	Aus.419774	RAAF		-
	W/O Brian D. Hawthorne	Aus.410662	RAAF		-
	F/Sgt Alexander G. Allen	Aus.428114	RAAF		-
	F/Sgt John R. Cunningham	Aus.430161	RAAF		-
	Sgt Noel E. Hunter	Aus.438333	RAAF		-
	F/L Edmund L.W. Ekert	Aus.404499	RAAF	A47-2/Z	-
	W/O Murray L. Tune	Aus.417434	RAAF		-
	F/L Leonard W. MacDonnell	Aus.404439	RAAF		-
	F/O John A. Bice	Aus.403999	RAAF		-
	W/O Earl L.F. Ralph	Aus.408781	RAAF		-
	W/O Charles A. Derrick	Aus.410638	RAAF		-
	F/Sgt William J. Hensman	Aus.431725	RAAF		-

TOTAL: 7

1 Armourer, was flying as extra crew.
2 Squadron's chaplain.
3 English-born Australian.

Aircraft Lost by Accident

Date	Unit	Crew	Service Number	Origin	Serial/Code	Fate
01.06.44	No.2 Sqn	*ground accident.*	-		A47-20	-
06.08.44	No.2 Sqn	F/O Stanley **Davies**	Aus.415512	RAAF	A47-13	-
		P/O Arthur K. **Buckland**	Aus.7010	RAAF		†
		F/O David G. **Lane**	Aus.416434	RAAF		†
		W/O John S.McL. **Campbell**	Aus.415227	RAAF		†
		W/O Arthur K. **Griesbach**	Aus.415321	RAAF		†
		Sgt Frederick H. **Conaghan**	Aus.433289	RAAF		†
		F/O Kenneth J. **Hadley***	RAF No.131581	RAF		†
11.12.44	No.1 AD	F/L Robert A. **Wines**	Aus.402432	RAAF	A47-24	†
		S/L Frederick R. **McGrill**	Aus.575	RAAF		†
		LAC Ronald J. **Cavanagh**	Aus.51756	RAAF		†
		LAC Denzil R. **Roberts**	Aus.84111	RAAF		-
		F/L Albert G. **Claire**	Aus.273495	RAAF		-
14.08.45	No.2 Sqn	F/L Edward M. **White**	Aus.402097	RAAF	A47-37/V	†
		F/O Alban K. **Morell**	Aus.7246	RAAF		†
		F/Sgt Bernard M. **O'Brien**	Aus.431510	RAAF		†
		F/Sgt Roderick A. **Macgregor**	Aus.433732	RAAF		†
		Cpl William J.C. **Maxwell**	Aus.34759	RAAF		†
		LAC Bayard A. **Marshall**	Aus.73231	RAAF		†
		LAC Victor A. **Morgan**	Aus.88726	RAAF		†
		LAC Ian S. **Coleman**	Aus.140811	RAAF		†
15.09.45	No.2 Sqn	F/L Lawrence A. **Kirk**	Aus.407439	RAAF	A47-19	†
		W/O Cecil R. **Ricketts**	Aus.429384	RAAF		†
		F/O Leslie **Bishop**	Aus.433889	RAAF		†
		F/Sgt Frederick J. **Stolweather**	Aus.439530	RAAF		†
		F/Sgt Ernest A.R. **Booth**	Aus.433083	RAAF		-
		F/O Peter A. **Taylor**	Aus.440106	RAAF		†
		Cpl Ray O. **Byrne**	Aus.33210	RAAF		†
		LAC Merlin S. **White**	Aus.141075	RAAF		†
08.10.45	No.2 Sqn	S/L David H. **Hannah**	Aus.404551	RAAF	A47-23	-
		No detail reported on the crew.				
12.10.45	No.1 APU	F/L John A.B.P. **Boyd**	Aus.400691	RAAF	A47-40	-
		F/L Keith H. **Taubman**	Aus.63342	RAAF		-
		S/L Allan M. **Stewart**	Aus.262713	RAAF		-
		W/O Alexander S. **Ross****	Aus.205623	RAAF		-
		F/Sgt Lloyd G. **Chapman**	Aus.47229	RAAF		-
		Cpl Ivo J. **Maher**	Aus.69951	RAAF		-

*Passsenger, pilot of No.549 Squadron, RAF.
**Scottish-born Australian.

Total: 7

End of the road for A47-40, seen here after its mishap of 12 October 1945. (*Aviation Heritage Museum of WA*)

TIME OF OPERATIONAL USE

SERIALS		DATE ON SQN	DATE OFF SQN
A47-1 :	2 Sqn [KO-Q]	28.06.44	25.08.45
A47-2 :	2 Sqn [KO-Z]	06.08.44	26.12.44
A47-3 :	2 Sqn	18.06.44	22.09.44
A47-4 :	2 Sqn (*see note**)	13.06.45	23.01.46
A47-5 :	2 Sqn [KO-N]	20.05.44	27.12.44
		03.02.45	27.09.45
		08.10.45	01.01.46
A47-6 :	2 Sqn	03.06.44	02.09.44
A47-7 :	2 Sqn [KO-S]	06.06.44	20.07.44
		11.08.44	01.09.44
		11.10.44	27.12.44
		16.02.45	04.09.45
A47-8 :	2 Sqn	18.07.44	01.09.44
		04.10.44	04.11.44
A47-9 :	2 Sqn	22.05.44	20.08.44
		09.09.44	30.09.44
		12.11.44	26.12.44
A47-10 :	2 Sqn [KO-W]	26.05.44	18.10.44
		26.11.44	11.06.45
		30.08.45	22.11.45
A47-11 :	2 Sqn [KO-C]	06.07.44	05.12.44
A47-12 :	2 Sqn	12.06.44	01.09.44
A47-13 :	2 Sqn	03.06.44	06.08.44
A47-14 :	2 Sqn [KO-F]	27.05.44	18.08.44
		26.09.44	01.12.44
		16.01.45	06.12.45
A47-15 :	2 Sqn	20.05.44	19.07.44
		26.11.44	25.11.45

A47-16 :	2 Sqn [KO-L]	25.04.44	19.07.44
		26.08.44	24.10.44
		16.11.44	23.02.45
A47-17 :	2 Sqn [KO-C]	25.04.44	09.05.44
		10.08.44	19.03.45
A47-18 :	2 Sqn	06.06.44	19.08.44
		08.09.44	30.10.44
		06.12.44	06.07.45
		08.08.45	25.09.45
A47-19 :	2 Sqn	26.04.44	20.11.44
		19.02.45	15.09.45
A47-20 :	2 Sqn	25.04.44	17.05.44
A47-21 :	2 Sqn [KO-L]	20.08.44	24.10.44
		08.12.44	17.12.45
A47-22 :	2 Sqn	24.07.44	10.10.44
		01.12.44	10.05.45
A47-23 :	2 Sqn	23.07.44	25.07.44
		14.09.44	23.09.44
		02.11.44	12.03.45
		13.08.45	08.10.45
A47-24 :	-		
A47-25 :	2 Sqn [KO-J]	29.07.44	05.03.45
		07.07.45	18.12.45
A47-26 :	2 Sqn [KO-K]	29.06.44	06.02.45
		23.02.45	09.11.45
A47-27 :	2 Sqn [KO-A]	29.06.44	31.08.44
		01.10.44	04.10.44
		08.11.44	13.02.45
		24.05.45	21.12.45
A47-28 :	2 Sqn	07.09.44	19.02.45
		07.06.45	01.01.46
A47-29 :	2 Sqn [KO-D]	20.08.44	21.12.45
A47-30 :	1 APU	06.03.45	02.10.45
	CFS	02.10.45	16.04.46
A47-31 :	2 Sqn [KO-P]	03.09.44	21.11.44
		11.01.45	21.12.45
A47-32 :	2 Sqn	19.10.44	08.11.44
		24.11.44	16.07.45
A47-33 :	2 Sqn	01.12.44	20.12.44
A47-34 :	2 Sqn [KO-E]	08.11.44	30.10.45
A47-35 :	2 Sqn [KO-R]	12.05.45	25.08.45
		04.10.45	08.01.46
A47-36 :	2 Sqn [KO-Z]	22.04.45	28.02.46
A47-37 :	2 Sqn [KO-V]	22.03.45	14.08.45
A47-38 :	CFS	08.10.44	09.04.46
A47-39 :	CFS	18.10.44	18.11.44
	2 Sqn	06.12.44	28.04.45
A47-40 :	-		
A47-41 :	2 Sqn [KO-U]	27.06.45	01.01.46
A47-42 :	-		
A47-43 :	2 Sqn [KO-B]	26.06.45	21.12.45
A47-44 :	-		
A47-45 :	-		
A47-46 :	-		
A47-47 :	-		
A47-48 :	-		
A47-49 :	-		
A47-50 :	CFS	16.01.46	08.05.46

Note : Regarding the code letters of No.2 Squadron aircraft, these are as known from surviving photo at a time and not necessary for all the time spent at the squadron. Duplicated letter usage is due to introduction of replacement aircraft.
*A47-4 : The aircraft status card indicates that the aircaft was issued to No.2 Squadron in June 1945 only. But No.2 Squadron ORB confirmed its presence at the squadron in June 1944, probably on loan from No.2 AD.

Known number of sorties completed by each Australian Mitchell

Serial	Individual letter	First sortie	Last sortie	Total	Op.hours	Comment
A47-1	Q	26.07.44	27.04.45	37	239.6	
A47-2	Z	09.08.44	26.12.44	31	201.0	Lost on its 32nd sortie
A47-3	?	30.06.44	16.09.44	23	144.7	Lost on its 24th sortie
A47-4	?	-	-	-	-	
A47-5	N	27.06.44	11.09.45	38	228.6	
A47-6	?	27.06.44	01.09.44	22	132.3	Lost on its 22nd sortie. TT : 337.0
A47-7	S	11.06.44	03.09.45	45	274.9	TT : 581.4
A47-8	?	26.07.44	01.11.44	9	58.0	Lost on its 10th sortie
A47-9	?	28.06.44	21.12.44	32	206.9	Lost on its 33rd sortie
A47-10	W	18.06.44	05.09.45	43	255.8	
A47-11	C	24.07.44	04.12.44	29	174.7	Lost on its 30th sortie. TT : 197.4
A47-12	?	17.06.44	25.08.44	12	73.3	Lost on its 13th sortie
A47-13	?	11.06.44	02.08.44	19	123.1	TT : 252.5
A47-14	F	12.06.44	21.09.45	44	275.0	
A47-15	?	13.06.44	14.09.45	32	184.0	
A47-16	L	17.06.44	18.02.45	57	349.5	Lost on its 4th sortie
A47-17	C	30.08.44	04.03.45	24	149.4	
A47-18	?	12.06.44	05.04.45	46	290.2	
A47-19	?	23.06.44	10.09.45	43	265.2	Lost on its 44th sortie. TT : 685.4
A47-20	?	-	-	-	-	
A47-21	L	25.08.44	21.09.45	35	206.7	
A47-22	?	26.07.44	01.06.44	39	244.9	TT : 435.4
A47-23	?	24.07.44	15.09.45	25	142.7	TT : 343.0
A47-24	-	-	-	-	-	TT : 87.4
A47-25	J	31.07.44	15.09.45	43	267.6	
A47-26	K	07.07.44	17.09.45	49	301.7	
A47-27	A	26.07.44	06.09.45	22	138.6	
A47-28	?	21.09.44	21.09.45	13	75.8	TT : 276.8
A47-29	D	09.09.44	15.09.45	33	209.1	
A47-30	-	-	-	-	-	
A47-31	P	15.09.44	25.09.45	38	225.0	
A47-32	?	27.10.44	06.04.45	19	119.8	
A47-33	?	17.12.44	19.12.44	1	7.7	Lost on its 2nd sortie
A47-34	E	12.11.44	08.09.45	19	113.0	
A47-35	R	19.08.45	24.09.45	7	49.9	TT : 375.5
A47-36	Z	-	-	-	-	TT : 517.1
A47-37	V	26.04.45	26.04.45	1	6.4	TT : 344.8
A47-38	-	-	-	-	-	TT : 103.4
A47-39	?	20.12.44	28.04.45	15	97.1	
A47-40	-	-	-	-	-	
A47-41	U	24.08.45	19.09.45	14	70.7	
A47-42	-	-	-	-	-	
A47-43	B	05.09.45	16.06.45	8	45.3	
A47-44	-	-	-	-	-	
A47-45	-	-	-	-	-	
A47-46	-	-	-	-	-	
A47-47	-	-	-	-	-	
A47-48	-	-	-	-	-	
A47-49	-	-	-	-	-	
A47-50	-	-	-	-	-	

†

ROLL OF HONOUR

Name	Rank	Age	Origin	Date	Serial
BISHOP, Leslie	F/O	20	RAAF	15.09.45	A47-19
BUCKLAND, Arthur Keith	P/O	24	RAAF	19.08.44	A47-13
BYRNE, Roy Owen	Cpl	23	RAAF	15.09.45	A47-19
CAMPBELL, John Samuel McClelland	W/O	21	RAAF	06.08.44	A47-13
CAVANAGH, Ronald James	LAC	34	RAAF	11.12.44	A47-24
COLEMAN, Ian Stanley	LAC	22	RAAF	14.08.45	A47-37
CONAGHAN, Frederick Hugh	Sgt	20	RAAF	06.08.44	A47-13
DAGGETT, John Francis	F/O	23	RAAF	22.09.44	A47-3
EASTON, Hilford Charles	F/L	30	RAAF	02.09.44	A47-6
FORSYTH, Leslie Thomas	F/O	22	RAAF	20.12.44	A47-33
GRIESBACH, Arthur Keith	W/O	22	RAAF	06.08.44	A47-13
HADLEY, Kenneth Joseph	F/O	21	RAF	06.08.44	A47-13
HARBERGER, Desmond Frederick	Sgt	20	RAAF	22.09.44	A47-3
HAWKINS, Albert Edgar	F/Sgt	22	RAAF	04.11.44	A47-8
KING, Gordon Sydney James	W/O	34	RAAF	02.09.44	A47-6
KIRK, Lawrence Arthur	F/L	31	RAAF	15.09.45	A47-19
LANE, David Gethen	F/O	26	RAAF	08.08.44	A47-13
MACGREGOR, Roderick Alister	F/Sgt	20	RAAF	14.08.45	A47-37
MARSHALL, Bayard Anthony*	LAC	20	RAAF	14.08.45	A47-37
MATHEWS, Francis Hubert	W/O	22	RAAF	20.12.44	A47-33
MAXWELL, William Joseph Carlyton	Cpl	25	RAAF	14.08.45	A47-37
McGRILL, Frederick Reginald	S/L	26	RAAF	11.12.44	A47-24
MILLETT, Murray Scott	F/O	22	RAAF	22.09.44	A47-3
MORELL, Alban Keith	F/O	30	RAAF	14.08.45	A47-37
MORGAN, Victor Allen	LAC	22	RAAF	14.08.45	A47-37
O'BRIEN, Bernard Michael	F/Sgt	20	RAAF	14.08.45	A47-37
PALFREYMAN, Richard Colin	F/Sgt	26	RAAF	04.11.44	A47-8
PHILIPSON, Keith Rutherford	F/Sgt	22	RAAF	22.09.44	A47-3
POTT, Arthur Edmund	F/O	23	RAAF	04.11.44	A47-8
RICKETTS, Cecil Roy Morgan	W/O	23	RAAF	15.09.44	A47-19
ROLFE, John Alexander	F/Sgt	19	RAAF	20.12.44	A47-33
ROWLANDS, Thomas Harry	F/Sgt	23	RAAF	20.12.44	A47-33
SELWAY, Jack Howard	F/O	30	RAAF	04.11.44	A47-8
SLATER, Allen Wallace	F/O	28	RAAF	22.09.44	A47-3
STOLWEATHER, Frederick James	F/Sgt	20	RAAF	15.09.45	A47-19
STORMON, John Francis	W/O	30	RAAF	04.11.44	A47-8
TAYLOR, Peter Alfred	F/O	20	RAAF	15.09.45	A47-19
THOMPSON, John Ernest Stuart	W/O	20	(NZ)/RAAF	20.12.44	A47-33
THOMPSON, William Frederick Elmo	F/O	29	RAAF	20.12.44	A47-33
WHITE, Edward Melville	F/L	33	RAAF	14.08.45	A47-37
WHITE, Merwin Stanley	LAC	20	RAAF	15.09.45	A47-19
WINES, Robert Alfred	F/L	28	RAAF	11.12.44	A47-24
WISNIEWSKI, Bernard Alwin	F/O	21	RAAF	22.09.44	A47-3
WORMAN, Harry Benjamin	P/O	21	RAAF	04.11.44	A47-8

*Born in Singapore.

Total: 44

An air to air shot of KO-D/A47-29, the only known Australian Mitchell to have received a shark's mouth.
(*Harry Rosenhain via D.Vincent*)
Below, line up taken at Sattler Field on 15 December 1944 when they were to provide an escort for Spitfires going to Morotai. Note that the serial of KO-S, A47-7, is not painted on the aircraft. Other points of interest are the tail turret and its 0.50-in machine gun which is visible on the first two aircraft.
(*Steve Mackenzie*)

Not all Australian B-25s were camouflaged, and at least four were stripped to bare metal including this one, 'V', which was A47-37. These aircraft were usually flown by formation leaders. *(Steve Mackenzie)*

In the last stages of the war the top turret, and fuselage blisters, were deleted to save weight. Note on KO-B/A47-43 the individual letter is repeated on the nose but painted in black and in white as shown on KO-M on page 20.
(Aviation Heritage of WA)

Line-up of some of Mitchells of No.2 Squadron : KO-S, KO-E, KO-V, KO-A and KO-G. This photo was taken at Hughes Field in the Northern Territory on 19 July 1945 where they were used in anti-shipping sweeps in the Netherlands East Indies (NEI) with considerable success. In July 1945 the squadron was preparing to move forward after months of inactivity but the sudden end of the war altered the plans.
(*AWM NWA0943*)
Below, at the end of the war No.2 Squadron was used as a transport squadron and its Mitchells were stripped of their armament as can be seen on KO-M. KO-M is an unidentified B-25J, but surely a former Dutch machine as the two Lend-Leased B-25Js are known to be KO-B and KO-U.
(*Aviation Heritage Museum of WA*)

A47-20 at Hughes on 17 May 1944. The aircraft was sent for repairs after being the victim of a ground accident on 1 June, but was written off and converted to components. Note that the RAAF roundel and serial have been applied but the painters have yet to delete the USAAF serial on the fin.
(RAAF official via M. Long/D. Vincent)

A line up of a few No.2 Squadron Mitchells while stationed at Hughes. Located inland from Darwin, Hughes was one of many airstrips prepared in the area, it had been occupied by No. 2 Squadron from April 1943. Like most airstrips, it was not far from the highway to make easy supply and communications.
(Aviation Heritage Museum of WA)

Three photos of Australian B-25Ds. Top. A47-14/KO-F taken shortly after entering service with No.2 Squadron. Note the individual letter painted in black on the nose. Middle. A47-21/KO-L in January 1945 with 14 bombing mission markers painted under the cockpit. Lower. A47-36/KO-Z, a late arrival at the Squadron stripped to bare metal. The only markings painted on this aircraft are the roundels and the individual letter on the nose.
(Top, via J. O'Leary/D. Vincent, middle, H. Rosenhain via D. Vincent, below Aviation Heritage Museum of WA)

A47-2/KO-Z became one of the last two Squadron's operational loss - fortunately without casualties. The aircraft is seen after the mishap.
(M.Long/D.Vincent)

B-25 Mitchell A47-29/KO-D with its famous shark mouth at Balikpapan, Borneo in 1945. Behind, KO-R can be seen.
(AWM P00630.010)

The wreck of A47-11/KO-C, the only known example of a No.2 Squadron bare metal Mitchell to have received full squadron codes.
(Aviation Heritage Museum of WA)

Above. Line-up of four Mitchells at the end of 1944. Included are A47-27/KO-A (see colour profile), A47-34/KO-E (see colour profile), KO-X (serial unknown) and A47-2/KO-Z which also had nose art. (*A. Prince/D Vincent*)
Below. A47-21/KO-L (see colour profile) and KO-G which is probably A47-19. The date at which it received nose art is unknown. (*H. Rosenhain via D. Vincent and Kirk family via D. Vincent*)

Above a side view of A47-31/KO-P, a B-25J (*H. Hope via D. Vincent*). Below, A47-34/KO-E a B-25D christianed "My favorite" (see colour profile). Bottom, one of the view natural metal B-25D A47-11/KO-C before it crashed.
(Aviation Heritage Museum of WA)

Interesting close-up photo showing the tail turret of a B-25D as operated by the RAAF. This turret appeared on late batch D-30 and D-35 aircraft and was sometimes retrofitted to earlier models. It was more comfortable for the gunner but did not offer improved firepower, still having only a single .50 inch machine gun. Nevertheless the aiming was easier comparing to the previous installation. The Australians did not have the opportunity to fire at any Japanese aircraft.
(AWM - NWA0945)

B-25D Mitchell A47-21/KO-L, No.2 Squadron, RAAF, Hughes (NT), Australia, January 1945.
A47-21 wears the Olive Drab with black under surfaces scheme. This was an RAAF modification of the original USAAF Olive Drab and Neutral Gray scheme.
Note the symbols of missions painted under the cockpit.

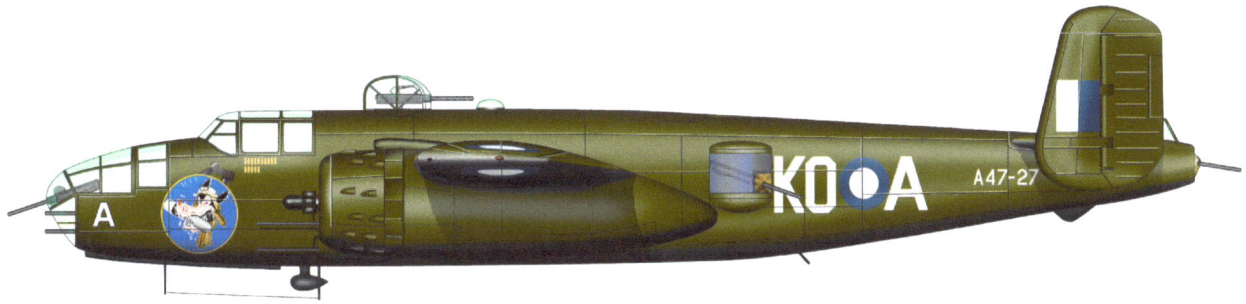

B-25J Mitchell A47-27/KO-A, No.2 Squadron, RAAF, Hughes (NT), Australia, December 1944.
A47-27 also wears the Olive Drab with black under surfaces scheme. Note the symbols of missions painted under the cockpit.

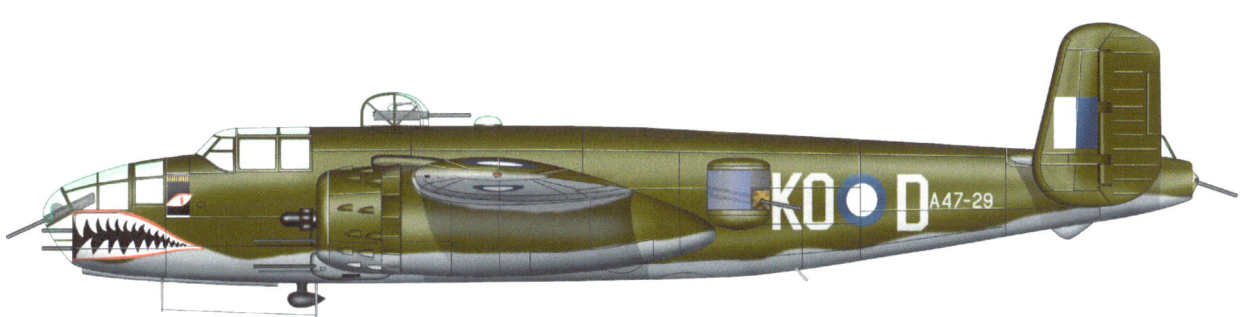

B-25J Mitchell A47-29/KO-D, No.2 Squadron, RAAF, Hughes (NT), Australia, August 1944.
This aircraft has the standard USAAF colour scheme of Olive Drab and Neutral Gray. This was the scheme in which B-25s were dilivered to the Australians.
Note the symbols of missions painted above the 'eye'.

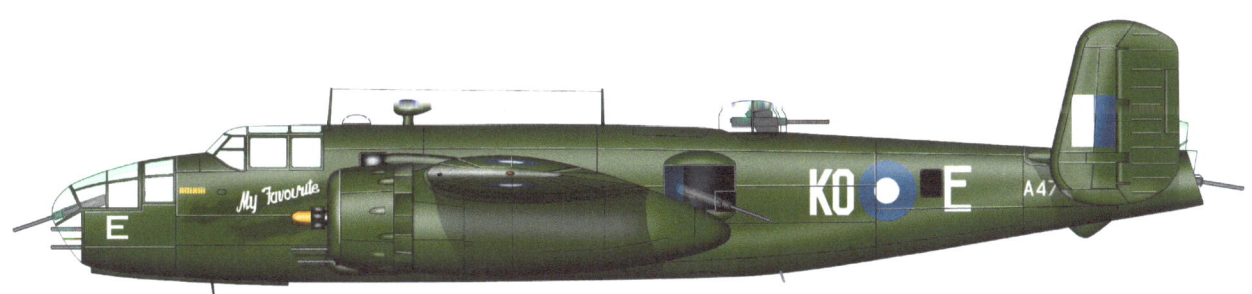

B-25D Mitchell A47-34/KO-E, No.2 Squadron, RAAF, Hughes (NT), Australia, March 1945.
This aircraft is painted withf the later RAAF scheme of Foliage Green overall. Note the late-war roundels with smaller white centres.
Note the symbols of missions painted on the nose.

www.ingramcontent.com/pod-product-compliance
Lightning Source LLC
Chambersburg PA
CBHW060802090426
42736CB00002B/129